Sidebox

Green

By
M Bowles

ISBN: 978-1-7331883-0-2

Publisher: Arrasa Press

For any inquiries regarding this book please email:
writeaway@fea.net

For
M and A
You've got this.

Other Works By M Bowles

Sidebox Linen Edition
Sidebox Blue
Finding Uncle Vince
Tolstoy's Mistresses
Tunnel Tramps
Horse Tails
Burning of the Bills
White Space

Contents

1-2   Catching Out Mr. Whitney

3-4   Catching Out: Train Hopping

5-6   Catching Out: Switched

7-8   Catching Out: New Orleans

9-10   Catching Out: End of the Tunnel

11   Tahoe

12   Polished Stone

13   Lower Chakra

14   Spaghetti Sauce

15   Cleaner Than a Hymn

16   Exhale the Past

17   Baptism

18   Clothesline

19-20   Farm in the Backyard

21   Mars Puppy

22   Puppy Obey

23   Subscribe to Your Life

24	Friendship Dishwasher
25	Sidebox 3
26	Hummingbird Nest
27	People She Doesn't Know
28	Lightbulb Burned Out
29-30	Grandfather Time
31	Running Out of Ink
32	Company's Coming
33-34	Planet in Handcuffs
35	Global Warming
36	Cat In the Box
37	Beyond the Shore Break
38	Beach Trash
39-40	Tributary Queen
41	Executive Extinction
42	Baby Mammal Fish
43	The Great Die Off
44	Octopus Mr. Eight Arms
45	Whichever Way
46	Barefoot on the Moon

47-48   The Argument

49   Belly Flop

50   Falcon in the Field

51   In the Salon

52   Am I Tired

53-54   First Flight of the Cooper Hawk

55   New Tenants

56   Zion in Winter

57   Vineyard Tender

58   Hitchiking

59   Sleeping with Words

60   Poverty of Vowels

61-62   Saleforce Tower

63   Pedestrian Down

64   Fire Alarm

65   Social Meania

66   Grand Old Parody

67-68   You Are Always Being Watched

69   Pouting Muse

70   Tweet Tweet

71	No Ropes
72	Dictators Do Best
73	Civics Sandwich
74	Girls Hang On
75-76	Madmen on Earth
77	Industrial Cross
78	Keep Us Safe
79	Hand Rolled Apocolypse
80	Fields of Hate
81	Ears to the Track
82	Rock This World
83	Conspiracy Theory
84	Where Were You
85	Refugees
86	Tormented Toddlers
87	Babies Cry
88	Poetry Pen
89-90	Orange Groves for Plough Shares

Catching Out: Mt. Whitney

He went to fetch his brother at the top of the mount
Highest in the lower forty
Bristlecone Pine below gasping for oxygen
Could only use binoculars
To admire the granite peak
All forehead and thin air
But the snowpack stepped a frosty foot
Across his way
Sent him back down the mountain
Only nineteen
Hitching the back seat of a VW bus
Along the spine of the I-10
Where the vapors hula hoop
The asphalt prairies of El Paso
And he heard his brother's voice when the
Train whistle ricocheted
Its call to the polished track
Broken rock back-slid his Vibram soled assault
Of the box car gathering to a gallop
Set his life's reach on the open slider, the pushup and high jump
He'd never mastered in physical education but did

In one leap of fear above the steel piranhas
Of the wheels gnashing below
Smacked his scraped resolution on the high platform
With no tears or forgiveness on his panting bruised back
The platform so high for so low in the lower forty.

Catching Out: Train Hopping

His mother's kitchen wrapped him in the oven mitt
Of warm banana bread
Settling his bruises against the grid of cardboard
Swaying as neat as the squares on a calendar
Empty of the dates in his mind that saw
He had never called home
Rattling further south of caring
To fetch his brother
But for the poison spiders the size
Of the candy bars in his empty back-pack
The man with the black suit coat
Who stepped from behind the banana boxes
Told him and squashed the hairy creature
Just getting to know his forearm
Where he crept into the far corner
Of exhaustion

There was nothing to rob him of but his mission
And he was beyond fear
Of the man whose face grew from the totem
Of the thunderbird named Bob.

Catching Out: Switched

His lurching soul was glad for
The cross-ties flat-sevening the wheels
In the syncopated jazz of his new fast forward
And the banana boxes
With the air holes onto his ripening
Next minute
The dust mote genies seducing
The sun through the crack in the door
And his head swaying
At the end of his neck
Until the motion
Fell onto its knees
Before the brakes
Decoupled his destination
From the future of his next move
And the line stopped its resolve
While the diesel engines made their getaway
Leaving a chain of box cars and flat beds
A mile long without pursuit
And the gold syrup prairie spilled across
The table of nowhere
Only the grin
Of wind bowing the desolate grass in a pageant

Pointing to his next move
A leap into the hope of his boots
Towards the big bosomed horizon
Blocked hard by the grip on his shoulder
The shake of the totem head
She'll bleach your bones in her cleavage
With no mal-intent
Stay in the shade of your precinct
The track vibrates with the engines
Hastening to couple the destination of your brother
And they sat to their near death for 36 hours
In God's hot breath
Though death never crossed his mind.

Catching Out: New Orleans

A panhandler plies his sainthood
Three rungs down
By squeezing the juice from strangers
Unlike a gentleman of the rails like Bob
Who reveled in his own resources
Dipping a comb in a pocketed jar of water
Run through his hair
When the time called for a leap of faith
Jump Bob said and jumped
A fine Cherokee from Oklahoma
Who could teach a nineteen-year-old to break
The void above the rushing ground
Roll on his fear
Dust the speck of dirt from his suit coat
Just a mile north of the city
Where a man could brew
A mean cup of Joe through a pair of women's hose
And coffee grounds dredged
From the dumpster fire in a soup can of water
Near the center of New Orleans
Where he went to fetch his brother
Which is where the new engines took them
The kindness brewing in the bowl of gumbo

Through the screen door back step of the club
Where he lost his heart to jazz
And almost the boots off his exhaustion
In the night
To the panhandlers in the park
Who would have just as soon slit his throat
Were it not for Bob sitting vigil
Turning him to the bus station where he found
A locker and a day job building fences
And enough change to call his mother
Although he never had fetched his brother.

Catching Out: End of the Tunnel

———————

Only after he had lived
With his bare feet on the slippery rocks
Finding some purchase
On the foothold of his journey
As the years crept their moss underfoot
And he stopped visiting his brother's grave
Under the California Oak behind the church
Floated his wife's ashes of fifty years
Along the alpine pool
Where they skinny-dipped their young love
Into three fine children who each
Crested Whitney of their own right
Only when what was left of their earthly union
Had swirled into the clitter-clatter
Of the runaway creek dead set on the sea
Did he hear the far-off whistle of the freight train
Entering the tunnel at the top of the grade
And in an instant of the breeze catching its breath

The polished track vibrated in his veins
The totem face rose above the black suit-coat
So many revolutions of the wheels ago
Only then did he see
Bob was the brother sent to fetch him.

Tahoe

I only asked for the key to the laundry room
Not your heart
From the woman who read the future in the ice cubes
Of your glass as it hit the table
And my footsteps on the stairs of the
Chestnut horse we named under the snowfall
Where the balloon bumped its head at you from the high rafters
As you tried to land it with your sweatshirt
Flung beneath
My father's frown
We were witnesses to our wedding
Photographers and musicians
And the golden Eagle who officiated
From the highest branch of the white fir tree.

Polished Stone

What is this polished stone
You brought to me
In the palm of your calloused soul
From the clear river-bottom of a tributary
Beyond mine but so close to the bank
I knew its oval shape and brown speckle
As if I had smoothed it with my current
Before it left its place
Where the trout waits for the fly
In the shade below the riffles
And the waters fray and trickle close
On their barefoot path
Resisting
Resisting
Until the eyes bubbling on the surface
The ones who calculate the clear deeps
And know when it is time for the stone
To let go and flow to the sea.

Lower Chakra

———————

Do not bring those hips near
My dear

I do not need to bend your will
Around my waist

Yet those loins in the mirror

Bring your hips near
My dear.

Spaghetti Sauce

I love the red aria and the softening green notes
In the stockpot your song steaming
Garlic and rhyme circle the wooden spoon
Of your baritone
A child then two hover at your leg
For a taste
Of the seductive potion
We say were the cause of their existence
The pine trees shade the pinch of sugar
Through the lace curtains
While summer shuts the screen door on
The octave of your magic ingredient
Passed by whisper of an Italian boxer.

Cleaner Than a Hymn

He wiped the alleluia off his hands
And stepped across the chambers of her heart
To build a speckled life
In the sway of the olive ranch
Where the sonnet ran more clean and honest
Than a hymn.

Exhale the Past

Exhale the past
Let the children re-draw the petro glyph
On the ancient lips
With fresh chalk from the limestone
Hopscotch numbering
The hope of tokens
Plastic caramel-corn prizes landing
With two fresh feet over lost turns
I kiss the moon to sleep
Where it steals onto the forehead
Of your slumber so blue
I close your stillness
And breath the wonder
Of your existence
On the pillow next to mine.

Baptism

They lay the tiny creature of their love
On the green embankment of his conception
Inside a fawn morning
The holy water laying her fingers
On the sacrament of his forehead
As he gazed at the Godparents above
Shedding fond wishes from their evergreen canopy
The blue waving its sky welcome
Behind their branches sway
No clouds dared cross the beam of his vision
And even the harebells rang their tiny pink heads
On the exhale of his breath
There is a sacred stream in all of us
Born from the center of the earth
That wants to run clear and true
Against the flesh of gravity pulling us
Down the slope into the sea
It dislodges the speckled pebble who
Does not heed the brackish tongue
Lives on the creek bottom as pure as the christening
But volunteers for the journey
A polished friend small and round
As the infant's palm.

Clothesline

The art museum
Teaches us about
Going to the brave place
To hang your soul
With a clothespin
In the sun.

Farm in the Backyard

If you hadn't had a farm in the backyard
You wouldn't know the affinity of a rooster
For the back of a horse.

If you hadn't had a farm in the backyard
You wouldn't have seem him
Flap onto the chestnut haunches
Sprint his bantam feet
Along the sway of the back.

If you hadn't had a farm in the backyard
You wouldn't have known the big gelding
Hanging his head over the side fence
Turning his ears to your pitchfork
And gossip with the neighbors on the other side.

If you hadn't had a farm in the backyard
You wouldn't have seen the rooster
Scuttle up the staircase of the red mane
And drop his roost a horse-hair hat
Lording down on the dusty paddock.

If you hadn't had a farm in the backyard
You wouldn't have known the press of the city
Just down the street
Pawing and exhaling monoxide and grease
Launching winged spears into the altitude
To roar the rooster back into the coop
And remind you
That a farm in the backyard of a city
Is only a feathery dream.

Mars Puppy

Hello you big red cabbage
Mars in the southern sky
Mouthing above the August
Humid on my naked
Peeing of the puppy in the sleeping hours
When the moon slides cool
As a school bus across the ridge
Did the orange comb-over of your fury
Propel the Nazis boys from their bedroom war games
Onto the streets of the brown shirts
Buttons torn from purpose
What could they have made before
We infatuated with all things cheap?
Let the storks take them by the nape of their hate
Deliver them to their twin bonfire in the east
My puppy pees unsteady legs on the grass
His eyes only fill with love
And morning warm tongue
I am naked in the moon.

Puppy Obey

The dog pays close attention
To the eyes of the master
While the puppy points to
The spirit who
Vapors in the front hall
Beyond the reach of the
Weejie board
Raising the dead architect in the green
Chair with his glass of scotch
As he hand renders the underworld
Bracing the rooftop deck
On the back we build to the
Open sage of the canyon
Cart-wheeling to the palm-cupped
Sapphire of the sea
Good dog the puppy in the front hall
Nose raised obedient to the
Phantom glass
Of his specifications.

Subscribe to Your Life

Sorry
I do not subscribe to your life
It is bigger
Than the palm of my smart phone
Hello orange cat
With the nine moods
God is not the only one
Who knows every whisker
When you walk in the room.

Friendship Dishwater

How long have we washed each other's china
Known the easy move to the fill the basin
Find the plastic dish soap under the sink
With bubbles not words
The deep waters of friendship
Under the running faucet of the parent's
Fortieth wedding anniversary
The baptism and graduation
Before the sudden funeral of your father
Then your mother where the aunties nudged
Me away
We know the crystal pitcher bursts
When the rinse water is too hot
And the everyday glasses
Can overload the dishwasher
Oh how the dishtowels dry on the line
As the afternoon revolves around the sun
Yet there you are at the sink
When the wedding wishers overflow the brunch
And we laugh as I flip pancakes at the steaming griddle.

Sidebox 3

The sidebox calls to me
From its grave in the attic
Lid sealed against
The expiration date of childhood
O the diaries I must burn
Before the eyes of the children
The eyes of the children
The eyes of the children.

Humming Bird Nest

The shell of your tiny egg
Is as fragile as the rice paper
On the inside of my mother's wrist
Peering through the shades
At the nest you built atop the crown
Of the wind chime
Swaying on the breeze
Of ninety two years
Dreaming in the thimble
The motor of your buzzing wings
Silent as down
The lint from her dryer
Even a hair from her comb
And her softening heart
Mattress the nest
While my late father watches
From the other side of the screen door
Your little beak raises
A twig of hope
For one more year
Of tiny birds.

People She Doesn't Know

People she doesn't know
Visit my mother
As she dozes in her chair
Wearing bright patterns to match the wallpaper
If there were such a thing
In the apartment she has rented
Since my father got up and followed his ancestors
Into the other room
Classy people in classy clothes
For my mother I would expect no less
A short-haired women in a plaid skirt and cardigan
A man with a well-trimmed moustache
Friends her husband is sending
From the other side she thinks
And finds comfort in their company
While his ashes wait at the top of the bureau.

Light Bulb Burned Out

The elderly man has misplaced his sight
Under the dim of his electric bill
He searches for his horizon
Within the beam of the floor lamp
Beside his armchair
Recognizes the answer
To his crossword
Through the magnifying glass
And a flicker of the universe
From the television screen
Though he sits in the dark at night
For a week
Waiting for his nephew
When the light bulb burns out.

Grandfather Time

My grandfather wound his future
With a brass key
Christened the mechanism of time
Laid out on the garage workbench
Tiny springs and screws spilling from
The red tobacco can
With the royal visage
How could I know the import of his hour
With the time clacking its teeth
On every wall of the house he shared
With my grandmother
How could the tiny pendulums
Of the little bird houses
Out wag the serious schoolroom cadence?
They clap their hands in the same dance with the numbers
Though their choreography was a mystery to me
A grandchild running through the empty field
Dollar bill in my hand for the fast-food taco
My father would never allow
Slicing my foot on the jagged tip of my future
How could any of us know that the chimes and cuckoos
Would submerge into the worship of the smart phone
Who demands our time

And knows our secrets
The chimes and cuckoos who chorused the crescendo
Of my weekend sleepover
And that my grandfather gave to every guest
Until the walls were bare
And he was free to go.

Running out of Ink

_____

It takes a dying man
To read the verse
And write his thank you note
With a pen
Running out of ink.

Company's Coming

The card table tries to keep out of my way
Ducks its naugahyde head under the white linen
Ironed smoother than parchment
Alas the metal fold-out legs
Practicing modesty under the circular skirt
Where I crawl my three-year-old self
Underneath
Gaze up at the evil spring latches
How they love to pinch a thumb
While up top the sniffy Revere bowl
Proffers chocolate nonpareils
Looks down his polish
At the common spiral notepad
And pencil
Poised to note the "we" and "they"
The obvious overtricks, cunning contracts and
rollicking rubbers
For afternoon Bridge ladies with lipstick
So much weight to bear for a collapsible table
Of thin metal and plastic
And the pesky child beneath who knows the truth
About bare Sunday dinners of scrambled eggs
In front of the T.V.

Planet in Handcuffs

Look at you dropping plump grapes from the vine
Into my mouth
Even with wrists bound by barbed wire and coal
It's as it should be
My little planet in hand-cuffs
Don't pretend the fumes from my hairspray
Offend your delicate ozone
It was you after all who sent your agent
To muss my hair with his southwesterly fingertips
Or complain about the leaking pipes
Under your Montana creek
And the Indians camped out at Wounded Knee
Clear streams and natives are quaint memes
Blown by my jet stream across the prairie
So I can make my investor's meeting by noon
Do you really think you turn by sheer physics?
Do you know nothing about how the sun rises and sets
According to the mechanics of economics?
Or inertia?
The money does not trickle down like they say
It sits on its dead ass
Would languish in the landfill
With the Barbie carcasses and unmatched socks

Were is not for me
Bench-pressing the weight of commerce
Busting my pecs on your behalf I might add
Didn't I give you Earth Day and an electric car?
So a glacier or two have given up and dropped out
A few polar bears drowned
Aren't they supposed to adapt?
Look at me I am happy because the rising tide
Makes Cuba farther from Florida
Survival of the fittest as they say
Quit crying and use the Pacific trash vortex
To build a bridge if you must
I'm just about done with you anyway.

Global Warming

The sister in the doctoral program
Presided her clipboard
Over the empty swimming pool
Filled with animals
Chickens nuzzled the soft mouth of
The lion's mane
And the cougar forgave the mountain biker
He had just devoured
Within the perimeters of civilization
Unhinged
Beneath the watch of the frozen peak
Thawing
Joints loosening
Flowing their afterbirth into the sea
Rising to reclaim what always
Was hers.

Cat in the Box

Relax my child
Though the cat in the box is in short supply
Dead or alive
Only the computers know in their freezing baths
The sunbathing sea lion
Charges the dog on the sand
Does not know they are cousins
And the ocean mother calls him back
While an unmarked envelope lands on the driveway
In the middle of the night
We will not open it
Come into the wilderness
Where the truth runs cleaner than the wind
Lay yourself on the soft earth
Where we have smoothed you
A bed beneath the redwood
Although we will fade into the forest
Your existence bends towards itself
At the edge of the meadow
Where all questions will be answered
For you hold them all
Beneath the outline of your dreaming face.

Beyond the Shore Break

In this dog-eat-dog world
The blond retriever from the shelter
Heaves the wisdom
Of seven years to every one of earth's rotation
Onto the sand
Lowers her groaning joints
To groom the puppy so full of teeth and himself
Beyond the shore break
The dolphins sing their injured
Into the calm waters
The whale folds the diver
Under its fin to protect her from the shark
While the great sapien spurns the Bastille
Leaves the summit and the planet
In a hot rage.

Beach Trash

I pick up bits of trash
On the beach
Along with words
Even though
The Pacific Garbage Patch
Is bigger and saltier
Than my vocabulary.

The Tributary Queen

There was a queen
A powerful tributary from distant lands
Who rose and swelled
To cry her bosom into the sea every winter
Bringing with her a mighty legion of felled trees
In the current of her lamentations
But King Neptune was not impressed.

I rule seventy percent of the fifth largest planet
And more grains of sand than stars in the galaxy
He proclaimed and with a flick of his blue robe
Splintered her cellulose army upon the shore
Where humans built them into fragile hopes
And dreamed at night little knowing that the king
Was coming to claim more than the seventy percent.

As for you my queen
The king admonished
You have not the juice to fill my coffers
In the summer I will build a bank of sand
With my big toe to block your rosy hips
And your pelvis will parch away
While your thighs and sighs retreat into dust.

And so he did.

Executive Extinction

Retired oil company executives
Are washing up in glass houses
Overlooking the oceans they polluted
Throw not a rock through their window
Ye of the combustible metal animal
Guzzling their gas and galloping
Your economy on the bodies
Of lost dinosaurs
Dying their carbon extinction.

Baby Mammal Fish

Little baby leviathan
Bouncing on the knee of the flatbed
You little mammal fish
Red and blue caution lights of the police car
Flashing on the iridescent flukes of your tail
Almost touching the pavement
From out of your canvas shroud
Just a little baby not even a minnow tear drop
In the sob fest of the sea
Did you even get your first breath
Or did the weight of sorrow
Wrap your umbilical cord around its own grief
Where was your mother
Did she abandon you for the surface
To chase off a boat full of oglers
Smothering your first breath
Or were you just a still-born dream
Where the wave wept you onto the sand
The gleam of my front bumper
Not as luminous as your lifeless tail
Wending the canyon funeral
Up the drive where they rescue baby sea lions
But not a baby whale.

The Great Die-Off

These are polarizing times
But not for the polar bear
He is already sunk
On an ice cube sighing into the
Martini of the human morass
Who needs polar bears? Or tigers?
Or elephants save for their ivory?
What is the great die-off but another
Shade drawn
On closing time at happy hour
For the ocean, the jungle
Where the animated exodus
Snarls at your Teranasaurus Rex
And your human number is called into
The third ring of the circus
Stare into the plastic cup and know
You are just another
Empty straw in the fast-food doom
Of your existence.

Octopus: Mr. Eight Arms

How have you landed here my wise friend
Plated among the parsley and lemon?
Your salty mind and crafty legs fried to a crisp
In the pan
The gas burning its dominion
Over your intellect outpacing the whale
And many blood cousins I know
The coconut you take up in your eight arms
To tiptoe across the submerged sand
Then architect a safe shelter
Your heroic escapes from the laboratory aquariums
Worthy of a blockbuster
Your passion and family history
Sizzled into a French fry
They pass your plate but not the stories
The extra terrestrials who may have abandoned you here
No DNA upon those roiling fingerprints
Only the sweet of your flesh against our barbarous lips
How do we choose those smart brains to sacrifice
For the appetizer?
Even my leather belt had a mother.

Whichever Way

Whichever way, the shallow path
With the telephone wires asking to
Be buried under the asphalt
Whichever way, the shingled birdhouse
Where we can trade books
Like goodwill behind the glass
Where walkers look into the side yard
As young trees press new taproots against
The dry season and fire pants
Just over the hill
I hear the thirst of the coyotes
Who come down to lap
From my neighbor's fountain
The scrub oak plant their feet and know
That California was always a desert
The wagon trains are leaving for the north
As the cars circle the parking lots
Where there are no spaces
And the apartments rise on their hind legs
To balance on the colored ball
The ring-leader cracks the whip
What can we do but check the blind spot
And love our cars into the passing lane.

Barefoot on the Moon

The universe has a mouth
And it wants to speak to you
From the whale shimmering
Her wake of stardust
Trailing the ancient
Songs of the ocean through
The unknown value of a comet
Studded with precious metals
Un-mined by the brazen astronauts
Who know how to break gravity
With the hammer of their daring
Where my dreams can take me
Weightless from explosions of jet fuel
And towers turning to the earth
The fragile engines of man's ambitions
Jettison to bang their heads
On the laws of physics
While I walk barefoot on the moon.

The Argument

If you haven't heard the sea
Argue with the rain
I have

I made you the sea says
Glaring gray and furrowing his whitecaps
If it weren't for me you'd be just another clear day

Look at you lying there landlocked by the continents
While I have legs to dance across your solar plexus
The rain down poured

But what a waste pirouetting your patter
Water on water
When the almond trees are begging for a drink
I protested from shore

Quiet and run your dog, interloper
The wind hissed
Always trying to hurry the Cirrus message along

It was the rainbow who broke things up
Flexing right in God's face
One foot on the Inland Empire
The other igniting the ocean
Just where it falls over the horizon

Two white slivers
Who shouldn't be out in the storm
Turned their bows and raced toward it
To cast their lines
For a pot of gold.

Belly Flops

Not a good day for
Surfing -- waves belly flopping
On their own babies.

Falcon in the Field

I have sent my falcon out into the field
Look at the rabbit he has laid at your need
Do you not know you are hungry?
Will you let the grass grow to your waist
The carcass rot
And the falcon and I pass into the woods
Leaving only these feathers?

In the Salon

Beneath the ice
The river has a warm throat
She wants to dip in the sea
The woman with the Library of Congress on her head in foil
Wants to know where the beach went
While she was living in Texas
There is no longer a place for the lounge chairs at the hotel
We wear matching black robes
But are we even?
Is the masque to bring the bright back to my brunette
But a light show?
The pelican drops from the pink morning formation
And the sea will return the shore
In its own good time.

Am I Tired

Am I tired
Just bending my neck to
Look up at spring
All sharp talons and beaks
Pinned descents
Tiny heroes on the tail
Of raptors
Mouths like baby goblets
Screeching for the worm
Shaded from
The blue warfare of dogfights
Hawk, crow, kestral
Jeykl and Hyde
Protector and feaster of the
Nested tribe.

First Flight of the Cooper Hawk

How lopsided your first flight
Plummeting from the down of your mother's attention
The see-saw of gravity
Laughing up from the field
Until you find the gyroscope of your wingspan
And a solid fence that will answer
The first yawn of talons
Old enough to squeeze
The life from a mouse
Where you cling as if your life depended on the strength
Of its cellulose resolve
The breeze fussing the speckled dandelion of your breast
While you play fierce
Resisting the call of your father to the fragile branch
Where he would feed you a young lizard.

I should like to fly on new wings
With all the checkered feathers of hope
And beak as yellow as the morning
Hunting the wind
To lift me in its sacred circle
With my desire sharp-eyed
On all the small wakings of the canyon.

I have heard the cry of the hawk
How dawn flowed through your shadow
Sending even the smallest ant back into its hole
I watch, my feet heavy on the earth
Your dominion over the nest
And the blue trajectory of your freedom.

New Tenants

Dial 911
My new tenants in the Ficus
Are murderers
Felons from the nest
Sharp talon and beak
Savages with a
Wingspan that cuts
The song from the sky
Before the nuthatch
Even knows
He has died mid-flight.

Zion in Winter

It's endless, the red mountains, the purple geology
Stepping itself into the borders of the national monument,
On the glossy coffee table page
Hard outlined sentinels
Braced against time fleeing through
My window on the passenger side
And don't we love the holy outline of the anvil
The sky traces with its blue finger
Overhead the clouds run the relay
Knowing their time is numbered in raindrops
Though the wind licks your forehead
And the rivulets run between your toes
You do not blink
At the downward pull on my soft flesh
As transient as the morning.

Vineyard Tender

Succoring the tendrils wandering from their mother
On the vine
Blazing the passion back into the bunch
Just ripening into the flashing goblet
And the sun --
It started in the memory of a star
Who candesced its hopes
Against the supine canopy
With the explosion of will
Magnifying the prism
Of every human spark
On its way through the earth's casual breath
And sometimes you can see it play through the leaves
With the sharp-eyed emerald
Of a mischievous god.

Hitchiking

People don't hitchhike
Anymore
They take Uber.

D. Bowles

Sleeping With Words

You
My muse said
Passing the fig
Sleep with words
Because you
Cannot
Paint.

Poverty of Vowels

The unused syntax try to keep out of my way
They are but flab around the belt buckle
When I press "return" they have already vanished
Without a delete
Gone off to bedevil the journalist
Groping for a turn of phrase elsewhere on the planet
Too serious for a bluegrass-loving muse
While I sling my stew of alphabets
They find the byline in the dust rabbits under the couch of
Indiscretion
Where I have lain naked
On a humid summer plot
Only now I am related to the happy poverty of vowels
Climbing up the hayloft into the thin air of fine art
Where there is only straw not to be spun into gold
And empty of roosting geese passing eggs of the same element
Onto the award winning screenplay
It is all but false teeth
Bottle up the blockbusters and my green-eyed goddess
Store them safely in a cool, dark place
We suffer the brittle bones of the consonants
Yet you have never seen a cleaner verse tremble
Than when it lays its heart
On the soft bosom of an "a."

Salesforce Tower

What must it be like
To have sanctioned the skyline
With the bayonette of an idea
Higher than the torch of the Liberty Lady
Flickering from the other shoulder of the continent
How does it feel to change the forehead of the city
Because you are the tallest of the tall
In this brave and bawdy and hopeless city
So full of hope?

The clouds heel obedient at your waist
Fetch you little bytes
People too
Your blue ants
They spill from airports
To force their nature on every bar
And bed sheet.

What of you
The man with the mountain
Do you sneak up upon your child
Pull your past across the bridge
To catch the sun the moon the western shade

Shining on his profile
Catch him devouring
The limb of the bridge
In the vanishing point
Of the southern sky?
Gaze down on his uncircumcised tip
Throbbing dancing figures
From your place on the shoulder of God?

Like the first year I moved into my house
Befriended it from the grassy peak
Even stalked it overhead
From the window seat
Of a jet
Heading to Dallas.

Pedestrian Down

One siren cannot save the city
Rattling the chopsticks of your ears
Banging its head against the high rise.

The fire devoured the earthquake.

Who told the crosser his bone mass
Could out macho the lower lip of a bus?
The driver sobs on the curb
His boss just wants an affidavit
We stop to unnerve our hands
But the catastrophe gives us the finger
From the passing lane.

Fire Alarm

Children listen to
The artists and poets
They are the fire alarm
Chirping in the front hall.

Social Meania

You asked me to share my baby pictures
Connect me with
The womb of the world
While you lifted up the fluffy comforter
I shared with my lover
Unfolded every Valentine
Into a red, white and blue box with no top
One big party favor
For the red-flexor
Who supplied women
To wet the bed of our democracy
Without asking
You RSVP'd yes
To the invitation of their seductions
On the easy sheets
Of our ballot box.

Grand Old Parody

Government
Of
Putin.

D Bowles

You are Always Being Watched

You are always being watched
Put that price upon your head
Better to be safe
Than stumble around dead.

The camera on the light post
A few houses down the street
Watches for the speeder
Analyzes every license plate it meets.

A rock star's paranoia
Registers your face
Tags your social security number
Outside the concert space.

You are always being watched
By Kodak or the cop
So keep you hands above the wheel
In the traffic stop.

What about the laptop in the bedroom
The oracle you trust so dear
Cover his eye with tape
Or risk your naked fear.

You didn't know about the live feed
Perched on the nature hill?
Take that joint from your backpack
And you'll be paying your lawyer bill.

Suppose you run one thousand miles
Into the desert sand
Sister, you're even being watched
In the promised land.

For God looks down from heaven
Sifts through your every thought
Knows whether you're truly thankful
For that Mercedes you just bought.

Pouting Muse

My muse is pouting
Behind my e-calendar
And my bank account.

Tweet Tweet

The fate of the planet rests
On two hundred and eighty characters
In the silo of two-thumbed chirping
From the commode —
Off-the-duff emissions
That set the flock flapping
With no memory
That the birds out-sang the dinosaurs.

No Ropes

My muse sent me up
The wall of el Stanza
Without any ropes.

Dictators Do Best

Dictators do best
Just bare your teeth and beat your chest
No sweaty compromise required
Or halitosis of diverse brains wired
When you've got the army, police and bikers
Who has time for tree-huggers and hikers?
Sap the tedious brew of the melting pot
Pour acid on the gaping sore of differences fought
Salute a tantrum filling in for a speech
Coddle your golf clubs in the mansion by the beach
The hairy armpits of common good
Banished to immigrant squalor beyond the hood
Separate the kiddies from their moms – torture the swine
You're just keeping the shitholes in line
With a wave of your little finger
The corrosive wheels of justice do not linger
As for Lady Liberty – she can take a hike
Because you've got a chirping bird for a mic
And while the comedians make us all laugh
You've confirmed another Supreme on the wrong path.

Civics Sandwich

———————

Tuned out of high school?
Forget the tasty diploma
We are about to get a
Big civics sandwich.

Girls Hang On

Girls, hang onto
Your vaginas
And your charm bracelets
The Supreme Court
Is coming for them.

Madmen on Earth

Children your soft bodies
Cannot survive the napalm
Dropping from the lips of the madman
Who has co-opted a bird
To carry his bombs
Feathering the nests of soft minds
Hiding treachery
Behind the innocent chirp.

Madmen have roamed this earth before
They painted pretty pictures
And loved dogs
But we have not invented the time machine
To satisfy everyone's wish list--

There is only now!

The explosions rustle in their silos
Your bodies are soft
These pages will sift to ash
And the robots are not yet ready
To inherit the earth.

Industrial Cross

The cross has given up the steeple
For the industrial park
A cement tilt-up in the business
Of tending sins for cash.

Keep Us Safe

The towers are falling again
Into the nervous breakdown of our consideration
The balance sheets fluttering from the burst window
And bodies craving pavement for the fire
Alas, just bits of ticker tape
Losing against the contortions,
On the face of the grown justice
Crying over his high school yearbook
Acting-out against the smooth path foretold
A prophesy of cheaters' pool
That has made speed bumps
On the broken shoulders
Of a woman's courage
For the pale face daddies
Who will keep us safe.

Hand-Rolled Apocalpse

We commandeer
An autocrat from Pluto
To spare us from inhaling
The apocalypse
We hand-rolled ourselves.

Fields of Hate

I am learning to adjust my eyes
Before they scorch in the naked sun
Already I have seen history undress
And collapse under her own flesh
The raw meat of her hands cannot
Hold the door
Against the gathering march.

Ears to the Track

Put your ear to the track
Brothers and sisters
Hear the vibration
The boxcar of misery
Is at the station
It only goes one way
Into the mouth of the beast
There are those who have seen it
With their own scars
Tattooed onto the red beer-pong swastika
Fashioned from the hands of babes
Quick!
Tear the rails from their ballast
With your bloody hands if you must
Block hatred with the golden spike
Even love must rise up
On its hind legs and fight for her life
When the monster of hatred seeks
To tear the stars from the stripes.

Rock this World

An earthquake begins
At the core beneath the bare
Feet of the people.

Conspiracy Theory

The sea is full of space aliens
I've seen them on t.v.
They come with wings a flapping
Under the deep blue sea.

Where Were You

Where were you when
The jetliner flew into
The nervous breakdown
Of our world dominion
The can-do culture collapsing
Into its own hollow cheeks
The truth does not dance for
Political correctness
Or freedom of speech
It lives on the ancient tablet
In the deepest waters of the whale's song
The literate can read
The dark phantoms lifted off
On a runway of grounded planes
To bomb the school buses next door
While the busboy who
Perished with us in the ash
Is hunted across the border
His child abducted
By the star-spangled righteous
And traded for an unborn
We cannot say we did not know
We did not know
The boxcars led to the ovens.

Refugees

_____

We have colonized
Their homelands so now they are
Drowning for ours.

Tormented Toddlers

I cannot sleep
The immigrant toddlers
Torn from their mothers
Scream from behind their chain link
Into my pillow
They are my babies
They tug at my front gate
Lean to walk into my armchair
Chortle when I blow on their humanity
From the hidden prison
How are we marching
The goose-step we abhorred
In my third grade history book
Was our red, white and blue goodness
Just colored dye
And tearing a child
From her mother
Severing the righteous gristle
In the Big Mac
We call the land of the free?

Babies Cry

The babies cry from the cages
For their mothers.

But their mothers
Cannot answer them.

They have been banished
From the zoo.

Poetry Pen

Poetry is what
You would write
If you had a pen
When your muse
Washed up with the tide.

Orange Groves for Plough Shares

There was a backyard gate
That swung into a magic grove
Of forts and deep blue peacocks
Caretakers on horseback
Pulling the sun over their shoulders
To summon green buds from the branch
Until the bulldozers ordered
The oranges to sacrifice their juice
For your blood lust --
Missile sheathes turning on the lathe
And the perspiration of machines
Smelling of medals and power
Tipping the globe on its axis
And into your laps
Looping the cable of your will
Around the neck of history
Even the moon was yours
Smirking within reach through the
Upside down grove
Roots rising like the claws of dead chickens

Goodbye fruit fights
Vivid birds on the morning lawn
The blossoms sharing their sweetness
With the evening air
Only dust rising an apparition
My mother drew the drapes and wept
The gate was taken prisoner
By a chain link fence.

*9 7 8 1 7 3 3 1 8 8 3 0 2 *